Can You Go Fast or Slow?

Zachary Kolda
Elementary Library

Mary Elizabeth Salzmann

Consulting Editor, Diane Craig, M.A./Reading Specialist

Published by ABDO Publishing Company, 4940 Viking Drive, Edina, Minnesota 55435.

Copyright © 2007 by Abdo Consulting Group, Inc. International copyrights reserved in all countries.

No part of this book may be reproduced in any form without written permission from the publisher. SandCastle™ is a trademark and logo of ABDO Publishing Company.

Printed in the United States.

Credits
Edited by: Pam Price
Curriculum Coordinator: Nancy Tuminelly
Cover and Interior Design and Production: Mighty Media
Photo Credits: BananaStock Ltd., Brand X Pictures, Digital Vision, Purestock, ShutterStock, Stockbyte, Wewerka Photography

Library of Congress Cataloging-in-Publication Data
Salzmann, Mary Elizabeth, 1968-
 Can you go fast or slow? / Mary Elizabeth Salzmann.
   p. cm. -- (Antonyms)
 ISBN-13: 978-1-59928-715-7
 ISBN-10: 1-59928-715-3
 1. English language--Synonyms and antonyms--Juvenile literature. I. Title.

PE1591.S254 2007
428.1--dc22

2006032019

SandCastle™ books are created by a professional team of educators, reading specialists, and content developers around five essential components—phonemic awareness, phonics, vocabulary, text comprehension, and fluency—to assist young readers as they develop reading skills and strategies and increase their general knowledge. All books are written, reviewed, and leveled for guided reading, early reading intervention, and Accelerated Reader® programs for use in shared, guided, and independent reading and writing activities to support a balanced approach to literacy instruction.

Let Us Know

SandCastle would like to hear your stories about reading this book. What is your favorite page? Was there something hard that you needed help with? Share the ups and downs of learning to read. We want to hear from you! To get posted on the ABDO Publishing Company Web site, send us e-mail at:

sandcastle@abdopublishing.com

SandCastle Level: Transitional

Antonyms are words that have opposite meanings.

Here is a good way to remember what an antonym is:

antonym

=

opposite

Also, **antonym** and **opposite** both start with vowels.

antonyms

James skis fast down the hill.

antonyms

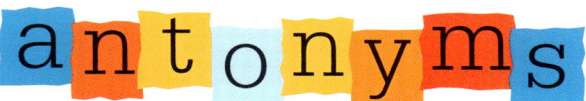

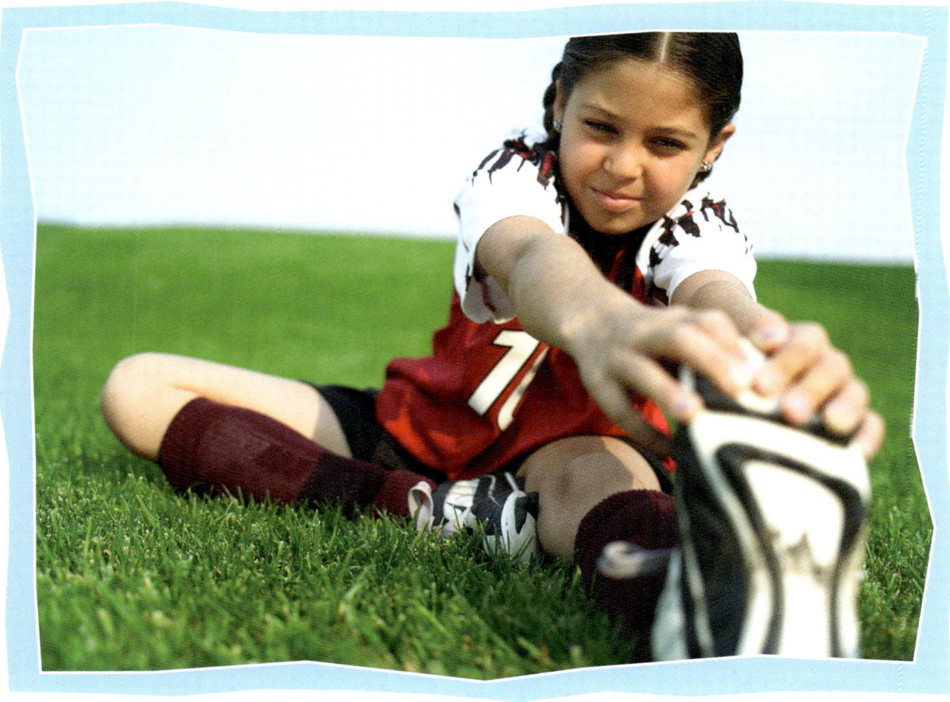

Alyssa does some slow stretches before her soccer game.

antonyms

Chloe and her parents wear hard helmets when they ride their bikes.

antonyms

In gymnastics class, Nathan does a somersault on a soft mat.

antonyms

Alex and his friends get ready to start a race down the beach.

antonyms

Jasmine is the first runner to finish the race.

antonyms

Rob, Gabe, and Tommy are on the football team. People cheer loudly at their game.

antonyms

Hailey is playing tennis. People talk **quietly** during her match.

In the winter, Hunter plays basketball inside. In the summer, he plays basketball outside.

Destiny is the first batter in the lineup. Her best friend, Kaitlyn, is the last batter.

Cameron practices driving the golf ball a long distance. Next he will practice putting a short distance.

antonyms

The basketball team is happy because they won the tournament. They played much better than last year, when they lost.

Antonym Activity

loud   quiet

finish   start

inside   outside

hard   soft

Antonym Pairs

fast — slow
finish — start
first — last
hard — soft
inside — outside
long — short
lost — won
loud — quiet

In each box on page 20, choose the *antonym* that describes the picture.

Words I Know

Nouns
A noun is a person, place, or thing.

basketball, 13, 19
batter, 15
beach, 8
bikes, 6
class, 7
distance, 17
football, 10
friend(s), 8, 15
game, 5, 10
golf ball, 17
gymnastics, 7
helmets, 6
hill, 4
lineup, 15
mat, 7
match, 11
parents, 6
people, 10, 11
race, 8, 9
runner, 9
soccer, 5
somersault, 7
stretches, 5
summer, 13
team, 10, 19
tennis, 11
tournament, 19
winter, 13
year, 19

Adjectives
An adjective describes something.

best, 15
first, 9, 15
happy, 19
hard, 6
her, 5, 6, 11, 15
his, 8
last, 15, 19
long, 17
ready, 8
short, 17
slow, 5
soft, 7
some, 5
their, 6, 10

Words I Know

Verbs
A verb is an action or being word.

are, 10
cheer, 10
does, 5, 7
driving, 17
finish, 9
get, 8
is, 9, 11, 15, 19
lost, 19
played, 19
playing, 11
plays, 13
practice(s), 17
putting, 17
ride, 6
skis, 4
start, 8
talk, 11
wear, 6
will, 17
won, 19

Proper Nouns
A proper noun is the name of a person, place, or thing.

Alex, 8
Alyssa, 5
Cameron, 17
Chloe, 6
Destiny, 15
Gabe, 10
Hailey, 11
Hunter, 13
James, 4
Jasmine, 9
Kaitlyn, 15
Nathan, 7
Rob, 10
Tommy, 10

About SandCastle™

A professional team of educators, reading specialists, and content developers created the SandCastle™ series to support young readers as they develop reading skills and strategies and increase their general knowledge. The SandCastle™ series has four levels that correspond to early literacy development in young children. The levels are provided to help teachers and parents select appropriate books for young readers.

Emerging Readers
(no flags)

Beginning Readers
(1 flag)

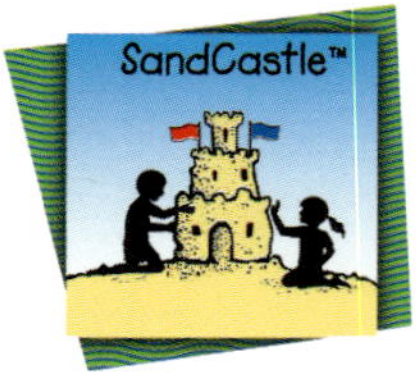

Transitional Readers
(2 flags)

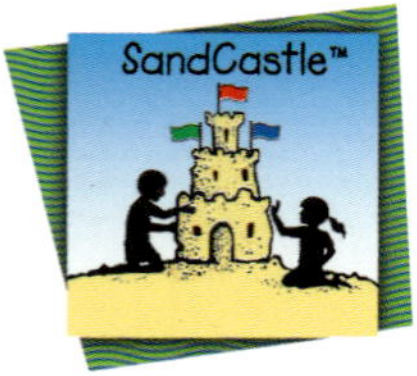

Fluent Readers
(3 flags)

These levels are meant only as a guide. All levels are subject to change.

To see a complete list of SandCastle™ books and other nonfiction titles from ABDO Publishing Company, visit www.abdopublishing.com or contact us at:
4940 Viking Drive, Edina, Minnesota 55435 • 1-800-800-1312 • fax: 1-952-831-1632